My Dog Thinks I'm a Hero

By
Thom Peterson

Illustrations by
Lisa Bohnwagner

Copyright © 2018 Hawks Eye Photo and Lisa Bohnwagner

For Heidi.

A Hero's Hero.

My dog thinks I'm a Hero,

a Superman of sorts.

She doesn't care I'm just a guy, with normal worries, faults, and warts, and all that other baggage with which we humans have to deal.

My dog thinks I'm a Hero.

I wish that fantasy was real.

My dog thinks I'm a Hero who can manage any trouble.

I hate to let her down.

She's too cute.

Why burst that bubble?

Let her keep her
vision of the world,
just as she sees fit.

My dog thinks I'm a Hero,

and to her, it's all legit.

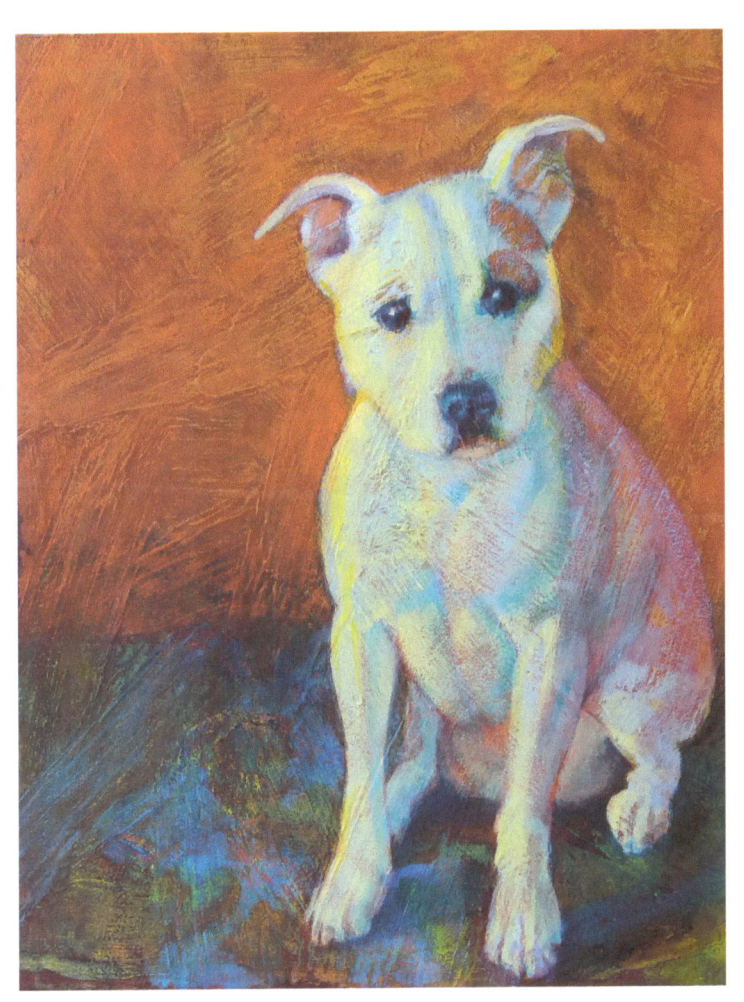

My dog thinks I'm a Hero.

Sometimes I'm not so certain she doesn't have me all confused with another person,

who could lay on hands
to cure disease,

or maybe...

...bring World Peace.

My dog thinks I'm that Hero.

Even when she's on a leash!

How does one live up to such

a lofty expectation?

I pondered this question.

Then I came to the realization,

that there lives a mighty Champion,

in every woman, child, and man.

Our dogs can see those Heroes.

So we must be Them.

And we can.

Thom Peterson lives, writes, and photographs from his home in Hixson, Tennessee. His passion for all three is inspired by his wife Anita, their four dogs and two cats. Four of the pets are rescues.

See more:

Hawkseyephoto.myportfolio.com

Facebook- @ThomPeterson

Instagram- @trp56

From her childhood on Boston's North Shore to her current home in the mountains of Georgia, Lisa has always expressed a deep empathy with nature.

"My passion is to express the wonder of it all, to foster a greater appreciation for the creatures that share our world."

See more of Lisa's work:

www.lisabohnwagner.com

Facebook: @lisabohnwagner

Instagram: @lisabohnwagner

Cast of Characters by Page

1	Emma	9	Boo Boo
2	Roxie	10	Vito
3	Lulu	12	Martini and Salvador
5	Max	14	Godiva
6	Heidi	18	Brassy
7	Jackjack	19	Betsy
8	Sally	20	Rex